GRIZZLY BEARS

by Kathryn Stevens

The Child's World

Published in the United States of America by The Child's World®
1980 Lookout Drive • Mankato, MN 56003-1705
800-599-READ • www.childsworld.com

PHOTO CREDITS
© Blaine Harrington III/Corbis: 7
© Bruce Coleman, Inc./Alamy: 20–21
© DLILLC/Corbis: cover, 1
© iStockphoto.com/Andrey Prokhorov: 3, 31
© Jeffrey Lepore/Photo Researchers, Inc.: 26–27
© John Shaw/Photo Researchers, Inc.: 8
© Mark Newman/Photo Researchers, Inc.: 25
© Michael T. Sedam/Corbis: 28
© Michio Hoshino/Minden Pictures: 17
© Robert McGouey/Alamy: 15
© Stephen J. Krasemann/Photo Researchers, Inc.: 11
© Steven J. Kazlowski/Alamy: 12–13
© Steven Kazlowski/naturepl.com: 5
© Stouffer Productions/Animals Animals–Earth Scenes: 18
© Yva Momatiuk/John Eastcott/Minden Pictures: 22–23

ACKNOWLEDGMENTS
The Child's World®: Mary Berendes, Publishing Director;
Katherine Stevenson, Editor; Pamela Mitsakos, Photo Researcher;
Judy Karren, Fact Checker

The Design Lab: Kathleen Petelinsek, Design; Kari Tobin, Page Production

LIBRARY OF CONGRESS CATALOGING-IN-PUBLICATION DATA
Stevens, Kathryn, 1954–
    Grizzly bears / by Kathryn Stevens.
      p. cm. — (New naturebooks)
    Includes index.
    ISBN 978-1-59296-847-3 (library bound : alk. paper)
    1. Grizzly bear—Juvenile literature. I. Title.
    QL737.C27S72 2007
    599.784—dc22   2007015285

Table of Contents

On the cover: This grizzly bear is warning people to stay away!

Meet the Grizzly!

Grizzly bears get their name because the tips of the hairs on their heads and shoulders are lightly colored. That gives them a grayish or "grizzled" look.

Up in the mountains, the sky is blue and the air is cool. A cold, clear stream splashes downhill through the trees and brush. Suddenly the bushes near the stream start to shake. Something is moving through them—something large! A big, shaggy brown head appears, followed by a huge, shaggy brown body. The animal sniffs the air and looks around. It lowers its head to the water for a drink. What is this big brown beast? It's a grizzly bear!

This adult grizzly is looking for food in Alaska's Denali National Park.

What Are Grizzly Bears?

People often use the name "grizzly bear" to mean all of North America's brown bears.

"Grizzly bear" is a popular name for a kind of brown bear. Brown bears live in parts of North America, Europe, Asia, and the Middle East. Scientists now believe that all brown bears belong to the same **species**. But people have given names to different types, or *subspecies*, of brown bears that live in different areas.

North America has two subspecies of brown bears—Alaskan brown bears (also called Kodiak bears), and grizzly bears. Alaskan brown bears are best known from the coast of Alaska. Grizzly bears tend to live more inland and are found all the way down into the lower 48 states of the U.S. The two subspecies are similar in many ways, including how they live. But Alaskan brown bears tend to be bigger because they eat more meat, especially **nutritious** salmon.

This female brown bear is fishing in an Alaskan river. How does she differ from the grizzly on page 5?

Grizzly bears are large **predators**. They're incredibly strong—and surprisingly fast for their size! In fact, grizzlies can run about 35 miles (56 km) an hour for a short distance. The fastest humans can only run about 26 miles (42 km) an hour. Male grizzlies often weigh 400 to 600 pounds (181 to 272 kg), while females weigh about 250 to 350 pounds (113 to 159 kg). Well-fed brown bears along the Alaska coast can reach weights of 1,500 or even 1700 pounds (680 to 771 kg)!

When grizzlies have all four feet on the ground, they stand about 4 feet (a little over 1 m) tall at the shoulder. But when they stand on their hind legs, they can be 7 feet (2 m) tall!

This huge grizzly is upset with the people nearby.

Like all bears, grizzlies are warm-bodied mammals that have fur and feed their babies milk from the mother's body.

One thing that sets brown bears apart from other bears is the muscular hump over their shoulders. These powerful muscles help the brown bears dig and hit with their big front paws.

What Do Grizzly Bears Look Like?

Grizzly bears' fur is especially thick and warm during the winter. In the summer, they lose a lot of this fur and tend to look shaggy.

Grizzlies have big feet! The tracks from their back feet can be 12 inches (30 cm) long and 8 inches (20 cm) wide. Tracks of Alaskan brown bears can be up to 16 inches (41 cm) long!

Grizzly bears are solidly built, with sturdy bones and heavy muscles. Their legs end in big paws with long, curved claws. Their thick coats make the bears look even bigger than they are. Other bears, including North American black bears, have faces that look straighter from the side. Grizzlies' faces are more "dish-shaped."

The "grizzling" in grizzly bears' fur means that their colors can vary quite a bit. Some grizzlies are blond or reddish blond, while others are light brown, dark brown, or even black. The grizzled hair is mostly on the bear's back and shoulders. From far away, grizzly bears look as though they have lighter-colored bodies and darker legs.

10

You can really see the "grizzling" on this mother and cub as they search for food in Montana.

Where Do Grizzly Bears Live?

Grizzlies once occupied 50 times more land than they do today.

Grizzlies even used to live on the vast grasslands of the Great Plains, where herds of bison roamed. The grizzlies probably liked areas near rivers and streams and fed on bison that grew weak or died.

Brown bears are found in many parts of the world, but the ones we know as grizzlies live only in western North America. In the early 1800s, some 50,000 grizzlies roamed throughout this region. They lived from the Mississippi River west to the Pacific Ocean, and from Canada south to Mexico. They lived in a wide range of **habitats**—rugged mountains, flat grasslands, forests, wetlands, and along the shore. As European settlers kept moving west, most of North America's grizzlies were killed. Farming, building, logging, and ranching also destroyed many of the grizzlies' living areas. Today, grizzlies still live wild in some areas. In the U.S., populations of wild grizzlies still live in parts of Wyoming, Washington, Idaho, and Montana. There are more grizzlies living wild in Canada and up into Alaska.

Here you can see a grizzly as it walks in Alaska's Katmai National Park.

12

What Do Grizzly Bears Eat?

Alaskan brown bears near the seacoast catch lots of salmon when the fish swim upstream to have their young.

In the Yellowstone National Park area, army cutworm moths land in large numbers on rocks. Grizzlies climb high in the mountains to eat the moths—some 10,000 to 20,000 of them a day!

Lots of people think grizzly bears are just meat-eaters. That's not true! They're actually **omnivores** that eat just about any type of food. In fact, they eat more plant foods and insects than meat. Their favorite plant foods include pine nuts, berries, mushrooms, and roots. They eat fish and small, ground-dwelling animals such as mice and ground squirrels. They also hunt bigger plant-eating animals such as deer, elk, mountain sheep, and mountain goats. In the spring, they hunt the young of these animals. Grizzlies also eat **carrion**, or the meat of dead animals. They even eat garbage from people's garbage cans and dumps.

This grizzly is feeding on a deer that was hit by a car.

14

How Do Grizzly Bears Live?

Some grizzly bears have been recorded as eating over 200,000 berries in a single day.

Grizzlies often stand up on their hind legs to see better and to sniff the wind.

Grizzly bears use their strong paws and sturdy claws to dig up plant roots and bulbs— and to catch prey.

Grizzlies are most active in the morning and the early evening. During the day they rest, often in sheltered spots. They usually live alone, except for mothers taking care of their cubs. Sometimes grizzlies gather together where there is an unusually rich supply of food. But when they're done eating, they go their separate ways.

Each grizzly moves around within a huge home range, traveling from one food source to another. For example, it might move to a good berry patch when the berries are ripe. To find food, grizzlies rely most heavily on their excellent sense of smell. Their eyesight isn't all that good, and their hearing is about like people's hearing. But they can smell rotting meat from over 2 miles (3 km) away!

These three grizzlies are all interested in the same thing— food! They are too busy eating to care that other bears are nearby.

In the winter, when food is scarce, grizzly bears go into a deep sleep for five to eight months. How long they sleep depends on how cold the winters are where they live. The bear curls up inside a cave, hollow log, or other protected den. Its whole body slows down to use less energy. In fact, its heartbeat might slow down from 70 beats a minute to only 10! Before winter, the bear eats extra food to build up a good layer of body fat. The fat keeps it warm over the winter and also provides energy. When spring comes, the grizzly bear is hungry! During its sleep, it has lost up to one-third of its body weight.

In the fall, grizzlies often stay active all day finding food, getting ready for their winter rest. They might eat enough to put on 200 pounds (91 kg)!

People often call the bears' winter sleep hibernation, but it isn't true hibernation. In true hibernation, the animal's body temperature drops more than a grizzly's does.

This grizzly bear is sound asleep in its winter den.

19

What Are Grizzly Bear Babies Like?

Female grizzlies tend to have a litter only once every three to five years.

Newborn grizzly cubs make a humming noise while they drink their mother's milk. Sometimes the sound is loud enough to hear outside the den.

Baby grizzly bears are called *cubs*. Mother grizzlies, called sows, usually have one to three cubs in a **litter**. The mother gives birth in her den, during her deep winter sleep. She does not even wake up when the babies are born! At birth, the cubs weigh only about one pound (one-half kilogram). They don't have teeth or much fur, and their eyes are still closed. As their mother sleeps, they drink her milk and snuggle in her thick fur to stay warm. When the cubs are about six weeks old, their eyes open. The cubs keep getting bigger throughout the winter.

This baby grizzly is just ten days old! Can you see how she uses her paws to cling to her mother's thick fur?

By the time spring comes, the cubs have teeth and a thick coat of fur and can follow their mother outside. The mother is thin and hungry from feeding those extra mouths during her sleep! The cubs keep following their mother around. They usually stop drinking their mother's milk when they are about five months old. But they stay with their mother until they are two or three years old. During that time, the mother protects the cubs and shows them how and where to find food. Once they are old enough, the babies leave the mother and go off on their own.

These grizzly cubs are four months old. They are trying to get their mother to play with them as they enjoy a sunny day in Alaska's Katmai National Park.

Sometimes grizzly bear cubs are attacked by wolves or mountain lions— or other grizzlies.

Almost half of all grizzly cubs die during their first year.

Grizzlies can have babies when they are four or five years old. They are fully grown by the time they are eight to 10.

Are Grizzly Bears Dangerous?

If you go to bear country, be sure to find out how to stay safe. Parks where bears live usually have lots of information about them.

If you see a cute little bear cub in the wild, stay away! The mother is usually nearby and will protect her cub.

A grizzly can kill a cow—or a person—with one blow from its huge paw.

Most of the time, grizzly bears are peaceful. But if the bears feel threatened or are protecting their cubs or their food, they can be very dangerous! Grizzlies—along with other wild animals—can also be dangerous when people try to feed them. And they can be a problem if people don't store food or garbage properly when camping.

When wild animals get used to being around people, they lose their fear of them. That can lead to danger! But bears that aren't used to people usually try to avoid them. If you're hiking in bear country, it's best to make plenty of noise. That way bears can hear you and get out of the way.

No one wants to be this close to an angry grizzly bear! Photographers use special lenses that zoom in on the bears from far away.

Are Grizzly Bears in Danger?

Grizzlies can live up to 20 or 30 years in the wild and even longer in zoos.

In 1982, thousands of Montana schoolchildren voted to name the new state animal. Their choice? The grizzly bear!

Although grizzly cubs are sometimes eaten by other predators, adult grizzlies have little to fear from any animal—except people. From the 1800s to today, most grizzly-bear deaths in the U.S. have been caused by people. Today, people live in so many parts of the western United States that there are few areas left for wild grizzlies to live. In fact, there are only about 1,200 to 1,400 wild grizzlies in the U.S. There are still thousands of grizzlies and Alaskan brown bears in Canada and Alaska.

This lone grizzly is enjoying a sunny day in Utah's Rocky Mountains.

Yellowstone National Park is one of five "recovery areas" where the U.S. government tries to preserve populations of wild grizzlies. In 1975, there were only about 136 grizzlies left in the Yellowstone area. That was the year the U.S. government listed grizzlies as "threatened" and took steps to protect them. Now the Yellowstone area has about 500 bears, and they are no longer listed as threatened. Even in Yellowstone, one of the bears' most important foods, pine nuts from the whitebark pine, is in danger. The trees are being lost to pine beetles, disease, and weather change.

Grizzlies will never be as widespread as they once were. But many people are working to preserve areas in which these big bears can live. That way North America will have grizzlies living free for years to come!

This watchful bear is one of Yellowstone's growing population of grizzlies.

All over the world, bears face another danger. They are killed for their *gall bladder*, a body part some people use in medicine.

Even in protected areas, people sometimes hunt grizzlies illegally.

In Alaska and Canada, where there are many more brown bears, people can hunt the bears legally.

Glossary

carrion (KAYR-ee-un) Carrion is the rotting meat of dead animals. Grizzly bears eat carrion.

habitats (HA-bih-tats) Animals' habitats are the types of surroundings in which the animals live. Grizzly bears live in a wide range of habitats.

hibernation (hy-bur-NAY-shun) Hibernation is a long, deep sleep that lets animals save energy to survive through the winter. Grizzly bears go into a deep sleep that is much like hibernation.

litter (LIH-tur) A litter is a group of babies born to one animal at the same time. Grizzlies have one to three cubs in a litter.

mammals (MAM-ullz) Mammals are warm-blooded animals that have hair on their bodies and feed their babies milk from the mother's body. Grizzly bears are mammals.

nutritious (noo-TRIH-shuss) Nutritious foods have lots of substances that animals' bodies need to stay strong and healthy. Some brown bears eat nutritious fish such as salmon.

omnivores (OM-nih-vorz) Omnivores are animals that eat both plants and animals. Grizzlies are omnivores.

predators (PREH-duh-terz) Predators are animals that hunt and kill other animals for food. Grizzly bears are predators.

prey (PRAY) Prey are animals that other animals hunt as food. Prey for grizzlies range from squirrels to mountain goats.

species (SPEE-sheez) An animal species is a group of animals that share the same features and can have babies only with animals in the same group. All brown bears belong to the same species.

To Find Out More

Watch It!

National Geographic Society. *The Grizzlies*. VHS. Stamford, CT: Vestron Video, 1987.

Public Broadcasting Service. *PBS Nature: Bears*. DVD. Chicago: Questar, 2003.

World Almanac Video. *The Grizzly Bear*. VHS. Beverly Hills, CA: Choices, Inc., 2002.

Read It!

Hirschi, Ron. *Searching for Grizzlies*. Honesdale, PA: Boyds Mills Press, 2005.

Shapira, Amy, and Douglas H. Chadwick. *Growing Up Grizzly: The True Story of Baylee and Her Cubs*. Guilford, CT: Falcon, 2007.

Stone, Lynn M. *Grizzlies*. Minneapolis, MN: Lerner Publications, 2007.

Taylor, Barbara. *Grizzly Bears.* Austin: Raintree Steck-Vaughn Publishers, 2003.

On the Web

Visit our Web page for lots of links about grizzly bears: *http://www.childsworld.com/links*

Note to Parents, Teachers, and Librarians: We routinely check our Web links to make sure they're safe, active sites— so encourage your readers to check them out!

31

Index

About the Author

Kathryn Stevens is an archaeologist as well as an editor and author of numerous children's books on nature and science, geography, and other topics. She lives in western Wisconsin, where she spends her spare time enjoying the outdoors, restoring a Victorian house, and making pet-therapy visits with her dog.

32